Perhaps You Can

Perhaps You Can

Poems by

Steven Deutsch

© 2019 Steven Deutsch. All rights reserved.
This material may not be reproduced in any form, published, reprinted, recorded, performed, broadcast, without the express written consent of Steven Deutsch.
All such actions are strictly prohibited by law.

Cover design by Shay Culligan

ISBN: 978-1-949229-85-1

Kelsay Books Inc.

kelsaybooks.com

502 S 1040 E, A119
American Fork, Utah 84003

For my wife Karen,
who provides constant encouragement.

With thanks to my poetry group
for years of good advice and friendship
and to Sarah Russell,
who was invaluable in organizing this book.

Acknowledgments

Eclectica: "Don't Get Too Comfortable," "Poet," "Summer Solstice," "Visiting Day"

Misfit Magazine: "After Tet," "New York City, 1968"

The Drabble: "Tea Ceremony"

The Ekphrastic Review: "Agnes Was Here"

Silver Birch Press: "How we grew"

Weatherings: an anthology of poems about homelessness: "Flotilla"

Word Fountain: "That Night"

Contents

I

My Argument with Thomas Wolfe	13
Don't Get Too Comfortable	14
For Sylvia	16
My Education	18
Tea Ceremony	19
Vietnam, 1968	20
Why I Am Not a Vacuum Cleaner Salesman	21
All you can Eat	23
How We Grew	25
That Night	26
Barry	28

II

Agnes Was Here	33
Poet	35
Flotilla	37
After Tet	38
New York City, 1968	39

III

Visiting Day	45
Father's Day	47
Thanksgiving	49
Summer Solstice	51

I

My Argument with Thomas Wolfe

Perhaps you can.
But hurry. Before dusk
grays your vision as your hair.
Before the asphalt buckles
with the weight of tomorrow.

Grab a Greyhound, man.
See America again.
Even if it's from
the worn and tired
seats at the back of the bus,
stale with the smell
of a million miles.

Just don't be surprised
when no one greets you.
The years treat memories that way.
You'll need to root around a bit
to find the ones that still say home.

Don't Get Too Comfortable

When I was five or six my brother told me
I was swapped at birth.
"Dad liked the idea of two boys,"
he said one night, in the tenement room we shared,
"so they traded my sister for you at the hospital.
Her name is Sheila and she lives in the Bronx—
up near Yankee Stadium," he added for authenticity.

As I grew, I realized how much that helped explain.
Good grades, good manners, good behavior—
just as the lack of schoolyard fights with razor blades
and broken bottles signaled my specialness
in a family where my brother's "work release"
was treated with all the significance of a Nobel Prize in Medicine.
When I was ten he told me, "Sheila is way smarter than you are.
I think my parents are having second thoughts." He was home
from the halfway house to reclaim nine-tenths of our room.

At fifteen, I thought I should ask his parents.
But that year I grew eight inches and gained
a nose and ears four times too large for my face.
With glasses, freckles, and red hair
I didn't need Aunt Kate to tell me,
in her slurried alcoholic murmur,
that I looked like no one in the family.
My brother wrote a lot that year,
on prison-issue stationery,
to remind me "not to get too comfortable."

At eighteen, I went away to school.
"To learn a trade," parroted my fat-headed Uncle Arthur.
His forty-year-old son, he often told us, made real good money
at the craps game at the local schoolyard.
"He knows to bring an extra pair of dice,"
he'd say to anyone who'd listen.
My brother sent a photo of his first-born girl.
"I've named her Sheila," he penciled on the back.

I found a hundred reasons to stay away from home.
My brother married and divorced on schedule.
The nieces and the nephews, whose names I barely know
are more numerous than the pebbles placed
upon the headstones set for Mom and Dad.
My brother took a third strike in 2006.
He writes to rant about the smallness of his cell.
We speak sometimes—rehash the better memories.
Each time I quiz him on my birth.
Each time he warns me "not to get too comfortable."
Each time I get to hear my brother laugh.

For Sylvia

I can laugh now,
but for a time
I was so scared
of my shadow
that I would only
venture forth at
night, or noon
or during an
occasional
eclipse of the sun.
You might guess
that I'd be ridiculed,
what with carrying
a parasol to school
on sunny days in Spring,
but my brother was
three hundred pounds
of muscle, hung out
with the Amboy Dukes
and carried, as a
weapon, half a tree
trunk like a third arm.
From the time I was
six years old, the other
children called me Sir.

My mother put an end
to it "toot sweet."
While no student
of psychology,
she took the time to
reason with me,
as she bent over a
steaming laundry tub,

in her ragged house dress,
like something out of Dickens.
She said quite clearly,
"Go outside right now,
or I will cripple you."
My mother never hit,
but I took my sneakered
feet down the tenement
stairs so quickly that they
barely touched the steps,
and then bareheaded,
I braved the April sun.

My Education

Grandma taught me to keep a kicker ace,
that post position trumped track condition,
and against all odds, to hit at seventeen.

She taught me to be leery
of one-eyed jacks, the queen of spades,
and politicians who found religion.
She told me often, and in crowds,
"That there moral majority
should mind its own damn business."

Grandma taught me to laugh out loud.
She liked to watch Fox News
and rail about the morons
in America. She'd howl with joy
when Bill O'Reilly "came on to prance."
She told me once that Palin had more balls than brains,
and could make her fortune dealing Faro in Las Vegas.

Grandma taught me I was lucky, so I am.
For thirty years
she shared a space with Mom
and Dad too small for three.
She never missed a chance to glare at Dad.

Grandma taught me
love is but a sprinter—lean
and easy from the gate,
but hate is built for distance—
surefooted, she will run,
and run, and run.

Tea Ceremony

Sunday morning breakfast
was as close as we
ever came to sacred
ritual in our house.
Mom slept in
and Dad would
orchestrate in
his best robe—
the eggs here
the butter there,
and the coffee pot
to the right of syrup.
He cooked the cakes
and bacon
in the cast iron skillet
his grandfather
had brought with him
from god knows where.

We ate
until our ribs ached,
until we could
barely breathe,
until the very thought
of rising from our chairs
was far beyond
our quiet contemplation.

Vietnam, 1968

When my brother held
me upside down
all the little lucky things
came pebbling out of my pockets
to land on the walk
outside the marble yard
on Hopkins Avenue.
I knew I'd never
get them together again.

It was not a sign
of his affection
that had me dangling,
shirt smothered, from my heels
in the Brooklyn sun.
It was a business proposition.
I was seven that summer.
He, a spry fourteen,
loved showing off for girls.
He'd ply me with action comics—
Batman and Robin,
Spiderman, and Green Lantern.
I didn't mind being dangled.

Things are simple at seven.
I found my two-headed buffalo nickel,
my bolts and wingnuts and the key to someone's lock.
My rabbit's foot had spun onto the straggly grass
at the edge of the street.
Fortunately, someone had thought to dye it yellow.
It struck me then that my brother should have it.
But, he had gone.

Why I Am Not a Vacuum Cleaner Salesman

> After "I am not a painter" by Frank O'Hara

Some people sell vacuum cleaners, door to door.
I do not. I was out late last night, celebrating
my 15th birthday with Richard Levine. We
set all the garbage cans behind the apartments
on Hegemon Avenue on fire. Today,
I skipped school and wandered the odd streets
of Brooklyn, seeking mischief. No luck. At noon,
I met Jacob G. and we had lunch up on the avenue
at Joe's deli. I had a couple of franks with sauerkraut
and a potato knish. I told Jacob about Rachmaninoff
playing in Irkutsk for Elizabeth Taylor. He looked at me
funny. Perhaps he hadn't seen the movie.

After lunch, I ran into Jackson P. and agreed
to meet him at the Livonia Ave. train yard that night.
Jackson P. is painting IRT cars. I'm often his look-out and
assistant—I shake the cans of dayglow paint. I met my
cousin Peter, and we took the train uptown to see
the Yankees play. We didn't have the dough so watched
from the elevated station. Mickey Mantle hit one
home run right-handed and one left-handed. I grabbed two
franks with mustard, at Nedicks, before heading home.

I stopped off quickly at Pier 41 to see my Uncle
Frank. It was deserted down by the piers and the ship,
The USS O'Hara, did not look that ship worthy. Frank was
deported to Ireland today, although he is Rumanian.
I waved but no one appeared. I waved again anyway.

I made it home before the others. My mom sells stuff
at Mays downtown, my dad pushes a cab around
Manhattan. My sister's studying somewhere to cut hair.
They trudged in tired and more tired. My older brother
came in after 8. He was carrying his vacuum cleaner sample.
It is heavy by 8. He didn't sell any at all today, or yesterday
for that matter. He didn't have much to say. We settled
down to franks and beans for dinner and tried,
blind tired, to find a warm spot to sleep.

All You Can Eat

Dad was banned for life
from the all-you-can-eat
places all up and down
the Eastern seaboard.
It was a wonder to see
his likeness on a greasy
"Not Wanted Here" bulletin
board at an Italian Smorgasbord
just outside of Dover, Delaware.
At 5-foot-two and 110 pounds,
Dad was a wiry, anxious man
of prodigious strength.
As a parlor trick, he would
rip a Washington quarter
in half lengthwise, while
downing a Bud. The eagle on
the reverse screeched like a
startled seagull as he pulled it apart.
The partygoers loved it.

I was there when he won
the Coney Island Hot Dog
Eating Contest in 1977.
He downed 51 dogs
in just under 10 minutes.
Unlike the other contestants,
who appeared hurried,
dad took the time to smear
a bit of French's yellow mustard
on each before devouring it.
The crowd loved it.

Now you folks all know
that I am just a faithful
chronicler of truth and beauty,
but I swear that on that splendid
4th of July, just an hour or so
after he ate a half a hundred hot dogs,
we got off the subway
a few stops early so Dad and I
could share a couple of pizzas,
at Gino's on Utica Avenue
with, of course, the works on top.

How We Grew

The summer I turned seventeen
a girl I never knew leapt from her 8th floor window.
She fell soundlessly
to land some twenty feet from our pick-up game,
just as Fox's one-hand set shot,
arced and graceful as a prayer,
clanged against the unforgiving rim.
My best friend, Red, threw up by the foul line.

It was a summer of sorting out.
In Vietnam, our country had need of its children.
Some of us—good at math,
good with words,
good at taking tests
went off to college—four years of a certain kind of diligence.
The others donned helmet and gun
and tried to make a deal
with a god they had no use for,
so that they might come home again.

I never knew what made her jump
on that perfect day in June,
when the wind, for once
blew from the north,
taking with it the stink of landfill
just five minutes south of us
in Canarsie Bay.
I often wondered just what it was
that defied her self-forgiveness—
how fortune shakes the die
in her palsied hand
and how we must learn to live with the lie.

That Night

"I'm sure there are good people out there,"
he said, as he eyed the door.
"I'm just not one of them."
He talked.
It was his way of calming down.

We were in a bar
up near Times Square.
You know the place
or someplace like it.
They serve boilermakers and boiled dogs,
and no, there was not a soul in the place
you'd want to take home to meet your mother.

The bleeding over his eye
was no better,
and the hand he used
to hold a wad of bloody napkins
up to the gash
was starting to swell.
Every time the door opened, he'd jump
and now he had me doing it too.

When we were young
and faced with something to bear,
we'd summon a magic
to make us invisible.
We'd close our eyes
and count to twenty-five.
It never worked, but it might have,
I closed my eyes.

The violence had been
rapid and real,
and I don't want to talk about it.

Barry

I made his bail
in some crappy
little courthouse
in the Panhandle.
I don't recall
the name for
what he'd sold.
The sun was high
and the light had
turned the town
an astonished white.
After, we ate
biscuits, eggs and grits,
drowned in the
deep red country
gravy so often
served in the South,
at an aging diner by
the railroad tracks.

We hardly talked
my brother and I—
our common past
as forsaken as
the tracks we sat beside.
He ate quickly, his
features flashing
lined and yellowed
in the dying fluorescent
bulb, half hanging from
a ceiling browned
with age and grease.
I watched in silence
as his forked hand shook.

Barry left
in the beat up truck
our mom had bought
him twenty years
ago, or so,
as I fingered the
keys to my rental.
The truck was blood
red once. We both
knew that he'd
jump bail.

I watched him
make his snaky
way to SR 20,
and then,
no wiser,
left for home.

II

Agnes Was Here

I saw Jay last week.
It was late,
and the streets surrounding
the intersection of the BMT
with the Church Avenue bus
were deserted.
He stood humpbacked,
sheltering from the snow
under the overhang
of the candy store that graced the corner.
The distance between us
had grown to a dozen years
and I thought to walk away,
but he stood blue
and shivering—fumbling
with a cigarette butt
he could no longer light.
We huddled over the subway vent
until the worst of the shakes passed.

He was years ahead
of his time,
in his artfully torn jeans
and army surplus jacket.
Who could have predicted
a generation would mimic his look,
if not his misery?

But he stole every show—
strutting the stage with his vintage Sunburst—
back when we were the next big thing,
before the booze
the smack
the nightly fights.

Back when we were family
before Agnes left him for the drummer—
the one we all called Einstein.

That graceless night,
I offered to find him shelter—
though he knew
I hoped he'd say no,
then slipped a few dollars
in his friendless hand
and boarded the empty bus home.

Poet

I found your first book today
in a second-hand store at the Harrisburg Station.
Dingy and age-tanned,
it retained its dustcover
with a photo of you at 22,
wearing a threadbare corduroy coat
I'm sure is still in your closet,
and what might pass for a smile.
It's a rare first print from '69.

My war.
Your deferment.
You kept to your poetry
like you kept to the old neighborhood,
both mired in bottomless poverty—
an endless scraping by.
Yet, just last year, *The Times* called you
the Bashful Bard of Brooklyn.

We will lay you out tomorrow
in a sandy plot
in one of those many cemeteries
that dot the flat, emptiness of the mid-island plains.
Bury you next to Mary
your common-law wife of fifty-three years
and your only treasure.

Old friend,
I never told you what I felt
when I first held a copy of your book.
I was outside my tent,
less than a mile from the wreckage of Ben Tre.

The package had been waiting for me
while we took that city down.
Not even the rats and the roaches
could have survived our fury.
"That should be me," I thought,
and tossed that splendid book
on the residue of the war.

Flotilla

You left behind
one half a jelly donut,
stale as last Wednesday;
some clothing, moth-eaten,
mildewed; two shoes,
one black, one brown,
with newsprint for the soles.
You left behind a paper sack
of winter warmth, and poetry
by Whitman, Poe and Crane,
well-fingered and browned in age.

You walked into the river
and left behind four dollars
and eighteen cents, which I
have spent on coffee
and a banana nut muffin,
that crumbled in its freshness.

Your poetry; penned
in your perfect prep school hand,
was stuffed inside two newish socks
atop the brown and laceless shoe.
It is unnervingly good,
but I can use the socks.
I crumpled your words in their freshness,
and set them to sail upon the river,
page by remarkable page.

After Tet

Rick got the glasses
in Tokyo, on R&R
and the shrapnel in Khe Sanh.
He said they turned sunlight
to a kaleidoscope of color,
and after the mortars
hit their tent at dawn
the ground about looked
like crushed strawberries.

That year, the Beatles left for India.
We sang of lonely hearts
and of fields that were forever,
while people took bullets
for their beliefs
or for nothing much at all.
The cities burned.

Rick said that he'd bought
the glasses
for next to nothing,
at a head shop
in Shimokita,
the coolest part of Tokyo,
because he could
no longer stand
to look
into his own eyes.

New York City, 1968

I.

When last we met
we sat on a stone bench
in Central Park.
Frost had put paid to summer
and the big trees shivered
in the tepid sun.
We fed a squirrel
the remains of your lunch.
You said the draftees
had left
from Grand Central Station
that morning—
your fallen face
the color of the gunmetal sky.
That winter the water main
broke on the avenue
that ran along the park.
For months, we had to take
the long way home.

II.

When last we met
we were in an apartment
in the East Village—
above the shop
that advertised "Fresh Produce."
You said the Weathermen
had blown out all the windows.
We sat on the floor
in the hellish heat
and the stench of overripe melon.

A cloud of fruit flies
thickened the air.
You said you no longer cared
to brush them away—
your face
the color of ripe honeydew,
your lips and eyes
covered in black dots
like a painting by Seurat.

III.

When last we met
we sat in a coffee shop
on 96th Street by the Y.
It was an hour past curfew
and we wondered how we would find
a way home through the mobs
and the frightened children
posing as soldiers.
Harlem was burning.
You said your family
had a dry-cleaning store there
and that hopelessness
was ingrained in the air and water.
Your dad kept a German Shepherd
as insurance on your livelihood,
but someone had poisoned it
with mock kindness and raw hamburger.
As we left,
they were pulling the iron grating
over the windows.
You went uptown.
I went down.

IV.

When last we met
we stood in a sodden graveyard
perched on a rise in Queens
that overlooked the skyline of the city.
The newly turned soil
screamed everlasting life.
You said your brother
would have been twenty-two tomorrow
were it not for the sniper's bullet
that hollowed his left eye
and blew away the back of his head.
I recited a meaningless prayer
in a language I had never bothered to learn.
We shared a cab back to town.
I got out on Sixth Street,
on the seedy side of The Village.
The steady drizzle
left room for only a meager sunset.

V.

When last me met
we stood at the bar
in Sonny's Place on Jay Street,
half hidden in the shadow
of the Myrtle Avenue El.
Sawdust coated the old oak floor,
the air heavy with smoke and sweat.
Sirhan Sirhan had just shot
Bobby Kennedy, his bloodied body

shown again and again
on the muted screen,
as if in one last replay
he might stand, shake his head, and smile.
Our beer staled in a silence
that might have gone on forever
had you not turned and left,
the door slamming shut behind you.

III

Visiting Day

I catch your smile
through the commotion
of that common room,
and I can see
my whole childhood in it.

Once, when our world was
just a stickball game
between the manhole
covers on Bristol Street,
you told me
there would be
time enough
for all things—
a tenderness to the phrase
so unlike you
and the life you've led
that I have carried it
as a counterweight of sorts,
to all your worldly transgressions.

Today, it's just the two of us—
as gangly and awkward
as the children we once were,
in a room filled
with the sound and smell
of misery, on a scale
I might never have imagined.
I have that, too,
to thank you for.
You shake your head
and laugh out loud

as if in explanation,
as the light fades
through the grim
barred windows,
on this, the last day
of an August
that has been
as hot as hell.

Father's Day

Your song sang in my mind today.
I longed so to sing it with you.
It was one of your sillier songs,
and it rolled round and round,
like that toy train you bought for me
once, when I was five or six.
It was more than you could afford,
and I soon disposed of it, as a child does.

I see you still, on that morning
you first walked with me to school,
New York City so slyly proud of
Autumn it cackled in the painted trees.
We sang together then and loud
and made a spectacle of us, you'd say,
like *Ben Hur* or *The Ten Commandments*,
screened in Technicolor at our theatre
by the elevated train. We made so little
from it, Dad—I have just the memory.

My cousins, my children paraded to your
songs. I suppose they sing them still.
But time sings in a minor key, wrapped
in weariness, as in a concert hall,
half full, on a gray and rainy afternoon.
The movie theatre has closed for good now,
Dad. Others share the sidewalks and the sun.

I realize now after all these years of passing
how much I took for granted,
and how little there is left of you

in the whirrings and stirrings of all
the lush, little lives of yet another spring,
and how very sad that must make me,
if it weren't for your song.

Thanksgiving

I picture you happy
and at the shore,
just a short walk
from the once fashionable resort
you may remember visiting
years and years ago.
It is off-season and
the corduroy jacket
you have worn forever
is not quite warm enough.
You hug it to you
with reddened hands—
a poor replacement
for the large brown buttons
you have never found
in all those years
of thrift store meanderings.

The storm that cat-whorled through,
as if confirming the season's demise,
has left the beach and small pier
you stand above in artless disarray.
A sailboat has been lifted from its mooring
and left upon the beach
like the plaything of a distracted child.
The waves will take some hours
to quiet, and the air retains
the faint taste of ozone
that brings a sharpness to your senses.
The red in the distant, cloud-free sky
promises a particularly fine morning.
It will break both clean and crisp.

I picture you happy.
I picture you
easy in anticipation.
The old coat slips
open, exposing
a lining matted
and yellowed with age.
Once again you glance
at your watch,
as if surprised to find it on your wrist.
A fine watch
of timeless design—
a gift perhaps from someone
who knew you
when such things mattered.

I picture your smile.
A fine smile—
a gift to those
who, over time, have cared for you.
Do you remember when that friend—
the one you have not quite forgotten,
said you smiled through your eyes?

I picture some good thing
coming this way for you.
Soon. Indeed,
in my picture,
it has already set out.

Summer Solstice

The last time I passed this way
my mother had smiled
and asked about the old neighborhood,
and I, wanting to please her,
dropped off the highway
and circled the streets of my childhood.
Today, as I turn off the parkway,
I am her age and alone.

The red-brick tenements,
that seemed to have sprouted
from these streets, have long
given way to monoliths
of poured concrete
and cinderblock—
warehouses for the poor.
And although the buildings
and the street names have changed,
this place will never be one that
people might aspire to live in.
Yet, I was mostly happy here,
sweating out my summer
days in that schoolyard.
I do not remember when we changed.

As I swing back on the highway,
the streetlights ease on, and the shadows,
destined to envelope this timeless place,
do, for one last time, gently fade.
And although the sun
may pause and retrace its steps across the sky,
I will not return to Brooklyn.

About the Author

Steve Deutsch lives in State College, Pennsylvania. His recent publications have appeared in *Panoply, Algebra of Owls, The Blue Nib, Thimble Magazine, The Muddy River Poetry Review, Ghost City Review, Borfski Press, Streetlight Press, Gravel, Literary Heist, Nixes Mate Review, Third Wednesday, Misfit Magazine, Word Fountain, Eclectica Magazine, The Drabble, New Verse News* and *The Ekphrastic Review*. He was nominated for Pushcart Prizes in 2017 and 2018.

www.ingramcontent.com/pod-product-compliance
Lightning Source LLC
LaVergne TN
LVHW091320080426
835510LV00007B/584